ROUTE BRANDING AND SPECIAL LIVERIES ON BRITISH BUSES

RICHARD WALTER

Front Cover: Twenty-one new, all-electric Switch Mobility (previously Optare) Metrodecker EVs entered service in 2020 – principally on the York Park & Ride network. This joint partnership between First York and City of York Council produced the first new First vehicles anywhere in the country since the company announced its commitment to achieve a zero-carbon fleet by 2035. 39514 (YJ70 ETE) was photographed operating the Monks Cross Shops Park & Ride Route 9.

Back Cover: First Aberdeen operates a batch of Wright StreetDeck FCEV Volvo Hydrogen zero-emission deckers such as 39706 (SV70 BXP), which also carries route branding for service 19.

First published 2022

Amberley Publishing
The Hill, Stroud
Gloucestershire, GL5 4EP

www.amberley-books.com

ISBN 978 1 4456 9643 0 (print)
ISBN 978 1 4456 9644 7 (ebook)

British Library Cataloguing in Publication Data.
A catalogue record for this book is available from the British Library.

Typesetting by SJmagic DESIGN SERVICES, India.
Printed in the UK.

Contents

Introduction 4

Arriva Blues and Sapphires 5

Blackpool Goes Palladium 10

The Greens and Oranges of Cardiff 12

Changing Colours in East Yorkshire 14

The Coloured Fronts of First Bus 18

Big and Bold Go-Ahead Group 34

Colours and Identities in Lothian 42

Limited Route Branding and Vinyl in London 46

National Express Numbers and Colours 47

Nottingham Goes Bright 53

Plymouth Citybus Flashes and Sparks 55

Diverse and Adventurous Reading Buses 56

Scottish Citylink Updates its Image 61

Old and New Stagecoach Liveries 63

Transdev Varieties 68

West Coast Motors Group Upgrades 69

Developing Shades of Yellow in Bournemouth 71

Bringing Back the Liveries of the Past 73

Liveries to Mark Special Occasions and Special Bus Features 84

Liveries for Hybrids, Electric and Gas Buses 89

Introduction

Those of you of a certain age will remember how colourful the liveries on buses and coaches were prior to the deregulation of bus services in the 1980s. With the formation of the 'big' companies, local identities started to disappear in favour of the now infamous Stagecoach stripes, First Barbie colours, Arriva blue and National Express white. Suddenly it seemed that great pockets of the UK lost their individual identities. Gone were the yellow and cream in Newcastle; green and white in Liverpool; green, yellow and white in Glasgow; and blue and cream in Dundee, to name but a few. A few operators retained their identities, but in general wherever you went across the country there were lots of similar colours and livery applications on the local fleets. This allowed buses to be transferred to other parts of the groups with little need for major change, apart from new destination screens and legal lettering. In central London the 'all red rule' meant that the appearance of vehicles became very standard, with companies like Metroline losing its blue relief skirting.

Gradually, the use of route branding became popular, with simple destinations on vehicle sides developing into more ambitious schemes incorporating vinyl pictures of local attractions and large route numbers and information. In more recent times, new livery applications making use of different colours for specific routes has given operators fresh and new looks. At the start of 2020, Stagecoach completely changed its livery colours: there were no more customary stripes, but there were separate colours for its long-distance coach operations.

When I first had the idea for this book, my intention had been to illustrate just how colourful the UK bus fleets had become; however, I vastly underestimated how many different liveries there were. So, I have attempted to highlight a hopefully good representation of some of the contrasting route branding and special liveries over the last five years or so in a variety of places.

To show how the full extent of current route branding works, I have included slightly more detailed sections on First Glasgow and National Express West Midlands, but other parts of both groups are also featured. Operators that are not part of the big groups, such as Nottingham Buses, Reading Buses and Lothian Buses, are illustrated too. It is now also practice for some operators to paint buses in retro/heritage-style liveries from the past, most of which suit modern vehicle types very well. A few of the many varieties from the last few years (past and present) are illustrated.

The tragic arrival of the coronavirus pandemic in 2020 has led to a very uncertain future for the bus and coach industry. In many cases dedicated route branding was thrown out of the window to allow the use of the most modern vehicles on critical emergency timetables. The troubled Covid-19 months are reflected in some of the photos featured.

My grateful thanks go to Andrew Chalmers, Chris Cuthill, Mark Lyons, Donald MacRae, Ray Parnaby, Gordon Scott and Alistair Train for providing some excellent photos. All are credited for their particular work. The uncredited pictures were taken by me.

Richard Walter
August 2021

Arriva Blues and Sapphires

Showing off an older style of fleet livery is Arriva Kent & Surrey Wrightbus StreetLite DF 1654 (KX61 LHW). It is branded for the X Bus 116 service to Hempstead Valley and shows some of the places it passes through in different sized fonts on the lower panels. (Mark Lyons)

In a newer style of livery, branded as Sapphire, is ADL Enviro300 2741 (CX58 EVN), pictured approaching Manchester city centre on Route 263. (Mark Lyons)

Arriva the Shires 6525 (YX17 NFC) is an ADL Enviro400 MMC with Sapphire branding for Route 320 to Hemel Hempstead, pictured in Sherborne Way, Croxley Green. (Mark Lyons)

Waiting time in York on Sapphire Route 415 is Arriva Yorkshire lowbridge Wrightbus Eclipse Gemini 2 1504 (YJ59 BTY). The bus was previously in the darker blue MAX-branded livery and registered AY04 MAX.

'Making your everyday journey sparkle' is the slogan on Sapphire Route 101 branded Arriva Kent & Surrey ADL Enviro400 6478 (YY14 WGC). (Mark Lyons)

ADL Enviro400 4408 (YX64 VMC) is operated by Arriva Midlands and seen loading up in a wet Birmingham on Sapphire Route 110 to Tamworth.

Arriva Midlands Volvo Wrightbus StreetDeck 4600 (FJ64 ETZ) arrives in the centre of Birmingham on Sapphire Route 110 to Tamworth.

Arriva North East VDL SB200 Wright Pulsar 2 1500 (NK12 FLM) on 306 Coastliner duties approaches Haymarket bus station in Newcastle.

Turning into Newcastle bus station is Arriva North East ADL Enviro400 7549 (YK17 NNZ) on Sapphire express Route X22.

The use of branding has its problems when route-specific buses might be required for other services. From the same batch as above is Arriva North East ADL Enviro400 6528 (YK17 NFF). Although branded for Route 320, it is seen at London Victoria on Route 758.

Blackpool Goes Palladium

Buses in Blackpool have been going through a transformation over the last few years. Standard vehicles appear in a corporate yellow and black livery, while in 2015 new Palladium-branded vehicles were introduced, including Mercedes-Benz O530 Citaro 554 (BJ15 UVW), pictured on Route 5 to Halfway House.

ADL Enviro400 City 407 (SN16 OVH) was another bus to enter service in Palladium livery with side adverts for routes 3 and 4 but seen here on Route 7 in the centre of Blackpool.

445 (SN67 WZK) was among a further batch of ADL Enviro400 City Platinum coloured buses arriving in 2017 carrying 'Love Your Bus' slogans. It is seen on Route 6 to Mereside Tesco.

Representing a batch of mini-ADL Enviro200MMC is Palladium-liveried 228 (YX18 KWH) on Route 7 to Lytham Saltcotes. Longer versions of these vehicles were delivered during 2019.

The Greens and Oranges of Cardiff

Cardiff Bus (BWS Caerdydd) are easily spotted in their bright green and orange colours. 552 (CN17 BGO) is one of ten ADL Enviro200 MMCs that are deployed on a number of cross-city services. It was photographed in the city centre on Route 23.

The Baycar identity worn by articulated Scania buses such as Cardiff Bus 603 (CN06 GDO) on busy Route 6 to Cathays Park.

Cardiff Bus operate a number of small Dennis Darts MPDs such as 188 (CE02 UUG), which carries route branding for Route X45.

ADL Enviro400 306 (CN65 AAU) was new to Cardiff Bus in 2015. It's bright and distinct livery stands out even in dull conditions.

Changing Colours in East Yorkshire

There have been a number of livery changes on the East Yorkshire fleet in recent years. From June 2018 the company became part of the Go-Ahead Group, which features later in the book. East Yorkshire (previously known as EYMS) operates as a stand-alone company within Go-North East. ADL Enviro400 MMC 923 (YX20 OEB) heads out of York on service X46 in the East Rider version of East Yorkshire's award-winning livery.

Go-Ahead East Yorkshire ADL Enviro 200MMC 396 (YX19 OVT) in the centre of York. It wears the most recent livery that is being rolled out across the fleet.

ADL Enviro400 795 (YY64 GWX) is a former demonstrator acquired by East Yorkshire along with other demonstrators in 2015. It is on Route X46 with a different style of branding and livery applied.

East Yorkshire B5TL eVoSeti Volvo 814 (BF67 GHZ) leaving its terminus in the heart of York shows off route branding for Route X46.

East Yorkshire MCV Evolution bodied Volvo B7RLE 383 (YX14 HDV) on Route 63 and seen in Moxon Way, Hull. (Donald MacRae)

MCV EvoSeti Volvo B9TL 793 (BP15 OLH) was the first such vehicle in the UK. It is another bus in the East Yorkshire fleet to be painted into the new livery and was pictured in Moxon Way, Hull, operating Route X46 minus any route branding. (Donald MacRae)

Pictured leaving Scarborough is Wrightbus Eclipse Gemini 2-bodied Volvo B9TL782 (YX14 HEV) with new livery and branding for East Yorkshire Coastal Route 13. (Gordon Scott)

East Yorkshire operate the Scarborough's Beachcomber open-top Route 109 to North Bay. Former London Abellio Wrightbus Eclipse Gemini 2-bodied Volvo B7TL 895 (LF55 CYY) is freshly painted. (Gordon Scott)

The Coloured Fronts of First Bus

ADL Enviro400 MMC First Bristol 33973 (SN65 ZDK) in First corporate livery but with an orange branded front, which is the style being adopted by most of the group companies. In this case it is on Route 1 but without specific branding. (Mark Lyons)

Another First Bristol vehicle. This one features a red front for Route 90, showing a frequency of every twelve minutes, and is Volvo Wrightbus StreetDeck 35142 (SN65 OMK). (Mark Lyons)

First West Yorkshire (branded as Leeds City) do things slightly different, having introduced a two-tone green livery with small coloured front areas. Showing a yellow front for Route X27 is Volvo Wrightbus StreetDeck 35265 (SL67 VWR). (Donald MacRae)

Similar livery but with a green front is First West Yorkshire Volvo Wrightbus StreetDeck 35577 (SK19 EZH). (Donald MacRae)

On service 54 with a magenta front is First Leicester Wrightbus StreetDeck Volvo 35187 (SK16 GVJ). (Mark Lyons)

Shades of blue and gold but with branding that is quite difficult to make out on the roof is 35162 (SK65 PWE) on Xplorer Route 376. (Mark Lyons)

First West of England have reintroduced the popular Badgerline identity. Looking very smart and colourful in a livery close to the original is Wrightbus Eclipse Gemini Volvo B7TL 32341 (LK53 LZB). (Mark Lyons)

A rather striking all-over blue livery for express link Route X10 between Cardiff and Swansea is First Cymru Scania KI14EB4 Irizar PB 23319 (YN55 PXK). The coach carries the name *River Ogmore* and initially carried Greyhound UK livery.

With the historic York Minster in the background, First York Volvo Wrightbus Eclipse Gemini B9TL 37067 (YK57 EZW) shows off the dedicated University of York Route 66 livery. Not every bus wears the identical style of colours.

Pictured providing the University of York Campus Shuttle service UB1 is First York Optare Versa 49912 (YJ15 AYO), also wearing a dedicated livery.

Twenty-one new, all-electric Switch Mobility (previously Optare) Metrodecker EVs entered service in 2020 – principally on the York Park & Ride network. First in the batch was 39502 (YJ69 CXC), which is seen by the historic York walls operating the Monks Cross Shops Park & Ride Route 9. A section on alternative-powered buses appears later in the book.

First Aberdeen triaxle ADL Enviro500 38224 (SN09 CDK) on 'The Bridges'-branded services 1/2, which serve Robert Gordon University as well as Bridge of Don – a five-arch bridge of granite crossing the River Don.

First Aberdeen operates a batch of Wright StreetDeck FCEV Volvo Hydrogen zero-emission deckers such as 39705 (SV70 BXO), which also carries route branding for service 19.

Originally numbered 69304 when new, First Aberdeen Volvo Wrightbus B7RLE 69354 (SV08 FHD) shows off the very attractive green and black Platinum livery for Route 12, 'Where every journey is a special journey'.

A colourful addition to the livery of First Aberdeen Volvo Wrightbus Eclipse Gemini B9TL 37635 (SV08 FXS). Aberdonian schoolboy Adam had his rainbow design paying tribute to NHS key workers during the pandemic brought to life by First Aberdeen, First Glasgow and First Midland (see also page 31).

Repainted from a dark, two-tone blue livery into the now more corporate style incorporating lighter blue for First Scotland East West Lothian service 23 is ADL Enviro400 MMC 33432 (SN66 WGC), which was photographed in St Andrew Square in Edinburgh.

For some years now, First Midland Bluebird buses operating to the University of Stirling have carried a special Unilink livery of rather bold orange and navy. ADL Enviro400 MMC Hybrid 39305 (SN65 CVM) is seen on a rather wet day in Stirling.

First East Scotland ADL Enviro400 MMC 39446 (SN66 WGY) – one of several to be given a two-tone pink livery for service 600 connecting West Lothian to Edinburgh Airport. The bus was pictured in central Edinburgh operating more traditional service X24 having lost its branding.

During 2018 and 2019, First Glasgow invested in a large number of new vehicles and revamped many of its routes by introducing specific route colours. During the pandemic in 2020, when special services and frequencies were operated, dedicated livery vehicles strayed onto other routes. Intended for pale blue Route 38 ADL Enviro400 34391 (SK19 ENF) on the X87 passes 34381 (SO68 HGC) on the X3.

Mustard livery for Route 3 as displayed by First Glasgow ADL Enviro200 Wright Eclipse 67821 (SN13 EBZ).

Fresh from the factory, First Glasgow ADL Enviro200 44673 (SK68 LYR) leaves ADL in Falkirk with red front for service 241 in Lanarkshire.

Also utilising the colour red for cross-city service 18 is First Glasgow ADL Enviro400 MMC 33265 (YX68 UPS).

First Glasgow ADL Enviro200 MMC 67022 (YX68 USY) approaches Buchanan bus station running unbranded on Route 87 but featuring a magenta front.

Blue fronted for Lanarkshire Connect service 240 is First Glasgow ADL Enviro200 MMC 67055 (SN65 ZDT) leaving Buchanan bus station out of service.

Turning into Argyle Street is lime green-fronted ADL Enviro300 67877 (SN63 MYX) on Route 2.

Yellow fronted for Route 75, First Glasgow ADL Enviro400 MMC 33209 (SK68 LWX) is about to enter service from Caledonia depot – the largest bus depot in the UK. In the background is a bus showing the blue branding for Route 61.

First Glasgow airport service 500 was revamped during 2019 and upgraded to new double-deck buses on a regular frequency from Buchanan bus station. Painted in a very smart purple livery is ADL Enviro400 MMC City 33107 (SK19 EOU). During 2020, when the restrictions from the pandemic led to a reduction in the frequency of the 500, a number of other vehicles in the batch were painted into normal fleet livery.

The Easterhouse terminus for First Glasgow Route 60. Wright Eclipse Gemini Volvo B9TL 37530 (SF08 SMU) displays the Covid-19 NHS key worker rainbow stripes designed by Aberdonian schoolboy Adam (see also page 25). (Andrew Chalmers)

Bold blue on Route 77, as shown here on First Glasgow ADL Enviro400 MMC 33393 (SK19 EOD).

Seen on a road test from the ADL factory in Falkirk is First Glasgow ADL Enviro400 MMC 34370 (SO68 HFP) prior to its branding for Route 38 being added.

In early 2020 First Eastern Counties relaunched its long-distance Excel route between Norwich and Peterborough. 36907 (YN69 XZL) is one of nineteen ADL Enviro400 City-bodied Scanias with diesel drives purchased for the service. The two-tone red with gold lining is very dramatic. (Mark Lyons)

An evening shot of 39485 (YN69 DTF), an ADL Enviro400 City Scania operated by First Bristol under the Metrobus identity on Route m3. (Andrew Chalmers)

Big and Bold Go-Ahead Group

With windmill in the background, Coaster-branded Brighton & Hove 939 *Edith Nesbit* Wrightbus StreetDeck Volvo (BX15 ONR) on Route 12A to Brighton. (Mark Lyons)

The extremely attractive Regency livery worn by Brighton & Hove Wrightbus Eclipse Gemini 2 Volvo B9TL 424 (BF12 KXB) *Havergal Brian* on Route 29 to Turnbridge Wells. (Mark Lyons)

A six-minute frequency is promised on Brighton & Hove Route 1, operated here by Wrightbus StreetDeck 810 (SK16 GWO) *Ann Quin*. (Mark Lyons)

Brighton & Hove Scania 719 (YP09 HWF) *Elizabeth Fry* is branded for Route 2. (Mark Lyons)

The distinctive Angel livery of Route 21 on Go-North East Wright StreetDeck Micro Hybrid 3 6319 (NK67 GMX) leaving Newcastle bus station.

Go-North East have introduced a number of eye-catching new gold-based X-lines liveries with colour area variations that have proved to be popular. Orange-themed ADL Enviro 400MMC 6353 (YX70 OKN) was pictured on service X84 to Hexham.

Go-North East Wrightbus Gemini 3 Volvo B5TL 6309 (NK67 ECE) has blue incorporated in its livery for the X21 service to Durham.

Go-North East 7153 (XL10 NCL) is one of seven refurbished Plaxton Elite-I inter-deck-bodied tri-axle Volvo B11Rs originally with Oxford Bus Company. It is seen leaving Eldon Square in Newcastle for Dalton Park on the X10.

Go-North East 6339 (YX69 NPC) is an ADL Enviro 400MMC that operates from Consett depot. It shows off the green design on service X30.

Displaying the red version of the X-lines livery is Go-North East Wright Streetdeck Micro Hybrid 3 6365 (NK70 BYB) from Washington depot on the X1 to Easington Lane.

When Green Arrows meet outside Central station in Newcastle. Go-North East ADL Enviro 200MMC 5490 (NK69 FBB), branded for Green Arrow Route 97 but working a Sunday service 12, passes two Lothian Country Green Arrow Plaxton Leopard Interurban Volvo B8Rs providing LNER rail replacement services from Edinburgh. (Ray Parnaby)

Go-North East operate a number of Quaylink services. Optare Versa 5388 (NL63 YAW) is by the side of the River Tyne on Route Q3 to Great Park and Ride.

During 2019 Go-North West introduced this new generic fleet livery to previously First Manchester-owned Wrightbus Eclipse Gemini Volvo B5LH 39215 (BN61 MWP), pictured at Piccadilly, Manchester. (Donald MacRae)

Oxford Bus Company Wright StreetDeck 902 (NK20 EKW) wears a dramatic black and red livery promoting designer luxury 'to get you in the mood'. The bus is one of nine originally intended for Go-Ahead East, but the batch was redirected to Oxford to spread resources during the height of Covid-19. (Andrew Chalmers)

All-pink Oxford Bus Company Wright StreetDeck 652 (SL15 ZGD) on route-branded City 5. (Mark Lyons)

All-yellow Oxford Bus Company Wright StreetDeck 682 (SK17 HHM) on route-branded City 3 promoting contactless payments. (Mark Lyons)

Colours and Identities in Lothian

Edinburgh Coachlines operate MCV eVoRa Volvo B8R SN19 FJA on service 13 in Edinburgh. The vehicle was previously registered 191-D-37522 with the Hilton hotel on the Holiday Inn Express at Dublin Airport.

Lothian Buses operate throughout the Lothian region, as well as within the city of Edinburgh, using different colours to a corporate style. Representing the traditional Edinburgh City fleet colours is another MCV eVoRa Volvo B8RLE – 74 (SJ70 HNK) – photographed on a spring morning at Olivebank heading towards its terminus in Musselburgh.

Lothian Country Buses based in Deans, Livingston, had eight 12.8-m Plaxton Leopard Interurban Volvo B8Rs delivered in 2019, which were branded as Green Arrow services EX1 and EX2. Both services had been withdrawn by 2020 and some of the coaches were used by the Lothian Motorcoaches part of the Lothian group. 9203 (SB19 GKG) was pictured in Dundee on hire to Abellio providing rail replacement services to Aberdeen following the tragic train derailment near Stonehaven in August 2020.

842 (MXZ 1752) (formerly SN57 DDL) was one of ten refurbished Lothian Buses Wrightbus Eclipse Gemini 2 Volvo B9TLs that operated with Lothian Motorcoaches. It is seen repainted in green and cream livery and approaching Wallyford Toll while on loan to East Coast Buses in April 2021. The high-back, luxury seats included for Lothian Motorcoaches have been retained.

Operating in territory formerly served by First East Scotland, East Coast Buses have depots in Musselburgh and North Berwick. Wrightbus Gemini Volvo B5TL 20005 (SJ18 NFV) was pictured at Wallyford Toll en route to North Berwick on service 124.

During 2021, Lothian Buses took delivery of eighty Alexander Dennis Enviro-bodied two-axle Volvo B5TLs. 623 (SJ21 MZF) was pictured leaving Wallyford on an evening rush extension of service 44 to Whitecraig in East Lothian. The corporate style of City livery appears on routes into many parts of East Lothian and Midlothian.

Lothian Buses normally operate three services to Edinburgh Airport under the Skylink banner. During the coronavirus pandemic in 2020, Wrightbus Gemini 3 Volvo B5LH 433 (SA15 VTM) was one of seven such buses transferred to Marine Garage for use on service 45, which connects Heriot Watt and Queen Margaret universities. It is seen approaching the latter at Stoneybank in Musselburgh. The buses later moved to Central for use on service 41 still in Skylink colours.

Following on from the delivery of the Lothian Buses triple-axle 100-seat buses, a subsequent batch were ordered for Airlink Route 100. ADL Enviro400XLB Volvo B8L 1139 (SB19 GNJ), seen on driver familiarisation duties, shows off the blue with red lining livery for these buses.

Limited Route Branding and Vinyl in London

Route branding in London is not nearly as noticeable as it used to be. A colourful exception was this livery (albeit without route branding as such) applied to East London Transit Wrightbus NRM LT942 (LTZ 2142) on Route EL3. (Mark Lyons)

Go-Ahead London operated this BCI tri-axle demonstrator TA1 (LX18 DGF) on Route 12 and the traditional red livery incorporates information on the features of the vehicle.

National Express Numbers and Colours

National Express have introduced a number of colourful brands across the UK. Seen in Birmingham is West Midlands Platinum Route 50 branded ADL Enviro400 MMC 6898 (SK68 MDV), which is named *Amee-Louise*.

There are a number of buses in generic unbranded Platinum livery that can operate as necessary on any route in the West Midlands area. Two such buses, led by ADL Enviro400 MMC 7509 (SK19 ETY) *Maddison Isla*, were pictured operating on Route 16 in Birmingham.

In the centre of rain-soaked Birmingham, West Midlands Platinum ADL Enviro400 MMC 6981 (SK19 EPV) *Alice Hope* sports joint branding for routes 82 and 87.

West Midlands Platinum ADL Enviro400 MMC 6747 (SN15 LJA) *Sadie Bell* on the X51 to Cannock.

The full-branded effect for Route 16 on West Midlands ADL Enviro400 MMC 6996 (SK19 ESU) *Varshana Ralh* on its arrival in Birmingham centre.

Some of the non-Platinum West Midland vehicles carry full branding too, or colour coding round their destination screens. ADL Enviro400 MMC 6120 (SN15 LGG) *Tina* shows this off on Route 126 to Dudley.

Generic West Midlands Platinum ADL Enviro400 MMC 6946 (SN68 MKC) *Sian Eugina Kathleen* heading to Solihull station on the X2.

Xplore Dundee (now owned by McGill's Buses) had two Caetano Levante Volvo B9Rs originally new to Kings Ferry of Gillingham in Kent for use on a service between Dundee and Edinburgh Airport, which started operating in 2019. One of these, 452 (BF63 ZSX), was pictured in its distinctive livery arriving at Edinburgh Airport. The route, numbered X90, is now operated by Mercedes-Benz Tourismos in two shades of green.

It's an all-green dark look for the Xplore Dundee fleet, with Wright Eclipse Gemini Volvo B7TL 7010 (SP54 CGK) showing off the livery that replaced the former white and red National Express colours.

The arrival of new ADL Enviro400Ms for Xplore Dundee in 2019 and 2020 saw lighter shades of greens being introduced, with coloured route branding. 6694 (SK68 MBF) is an example from the first batch delivered and branded specifically for Route 22.

ADL Enviro400 MMC 6882 (SN69 ZNU) from the 2020 batch received branding for joint Xplore Dundee services 5, 9 and 10. Contactless payments are encouraged, as the banner points out.

2241 (YX65 PXG) is an ADL Enviro200 MMC that was previously with sister company National Express West Midlands and transferred over in August 2020 before the operation was sold to McGill's Buses.

Nottingham Goes Bright

Nottingham City Transport (NCT) has adapted a number of different liveries on its routes, with several buses named after local people. It has also introduced a large fleet of biogas-powered buses such as Scania ADL Enviro400 426 (YP17 UFJ) seen on Route 10. (Mark Lyons)

NCT Biogas-powered Scania ADL Enviro400 447 (YN18 SXF) on Orange line Route 36. (Mark Lyons)

Showing branding for Bridgford Route 6 is NCT biogas-powered Scania ADL Enviro400 404 (YP17 UFD). (Mark Lyons)

Red line Route 44 is operated by NCT biogas-powered Scania ADL Enviro400 buses such as 413 (YP17 UGE). (Mark Lyons)

Plymouth CityBus Flashes and Sparks

Plymouth CityBus have opted for colour flashes to their route-branded liveries. Gas-powered MAN Caetano EcoCity702 (AU62 DWG) wears an OrangeFlash for Route 43. (Mark Lyons)

Plymouth CityBus ADL Enviro400 City 555 (WA17 FTC) carries an elaborate livery for Route 21A with SPARK branding. (Mark Lyons)

Diverse and Adventurous Reading Buses

Reading Buses have invested in a number of colour schemes for local routes and those into London and Windsor. Running on Route 17 is East Lancs Scania N94UD 805 (YN54 AEW). (Mark Lyons)

Another Reading Buses vehicle on Route 17 is Scania N270UD Omnicity 1112 (YN08 MMK), which is marked that it is powered by bioethanol. (Mark Lyons)

On Yellow-branded Reading Buses Route 26 is electric hybrid-powered ADL Enviro400 202 (SN60 ECX). (Mark Lyons)

Reading Buses Yellow Route 26 is being operated by ADL Enviro400 208 (SN11 BVO). (Mark Lyons)

Similar Reading Buses ADL Enviro400 755 (YX64 VRP), not actually on a Claret route but working a Route 702 into Victoria, London.

Reading Buses Purple Route 17 shows Scania Enviro400 City 717 (YP67 XCM). (Mark Lyons)

Wright StreetDeck 901 (SK66 HRR) ready to depart on Reading Buses Orange Route 12. (Mark Lyons)

Gas-powered ADL Enviro300 SG Scania K270 414 (YR13 PMV) on intriguing Tiger-branded Route 7. (Mark Lyons)

Having taken over Route 702 from First, Reading Buses chose to retain the Greenline identity but wanted a new application retaining the green colours. The first vehicle to receive the final impressive livery was ADL Enviro400 1208 (GO11 LDN), pictured by the Royal Albert Hall in London heading to Legoland.

Reading Buses trialled a number of demonstrators including Ensignbus BCI 301 (LX17 GKL), seen here in a green and silver variation of the usual blue and silver livery at Victoria, London, on service 702.

Scottish Citylink Updates its Image

At the end of 2019, Scottish Citylink introduced eighteen new Plaxton Panorama double-deck B11RLE coaches on the busy Route 900 between Glasgow and Edinburgh. The order was split between Stagecoach and Parks of Hamilton, who jointly operate the service. Showing off the revised Scottish Citylink livery with branding for the 900 is Park's HSK 651.

Another Park's of Hamilton Plaxton Panorama double-deck B11RLEs is LSK 871 in Citylink Gold livery, seen here operating on Route 900 and arriving at Buchanan bus station in Glasgow.

In 2021, Stagecoach East Scotland's Perth depot acquired a number of former Oxford Tube DAF-engined Van Hool TDX27 Astromega deckers, including 50261 (OW14 LJZ). This carries Citylink livery showing a map of the six Scottish cities that services operate from and to: Glasgow, Edinburgh, Perth, Dundee, Inverness and Aberdeen.

In early 2021 Stagecoach East Scotland's Perth depot also took a batch of ten Plaxton Panorama Volvo B11RLE coaches surplus to an order for the Oxford Tube fleet. Setting out from Edinburgh on the 909 service to Stirling is 50447 (YX21 NNJ).

Stagecoach also have Plaxton Panorama-bodied Volvo B11RLEs for use on Megabus services. 50411 (YX69 LCA), named *Aberdeen Angus*, was photographed leaving Buchanan bus station in Glasgow. Delivered new in all-over blue, this vehicle and others have had extra yellow added to the rear. The iconic driver and mascot Sid, who featured for years on all Megabus coaches, was sadly dropped in 2019.

Old and New Stagecoach Liveries

Showing off its attractive livery for the Cambridgeshire Busway is Stagecoach East 13905 (BU69 XYE), a tri-axle Volvo B8L with ninety-eight-seat ADL Enviro400XLB bodywork. (Mark Lyons)

Stagecoach Bluebird ADL Enviro400 MMC 11567 (SK21 FJZ) passes the impressive granite Marischal College, Aberdeen, in the current style of corporate livery shaped by customer research. which suggested a more simplified and modern service.

Seen in Newcastle is Stagecoach Busways ADL Enviro400MMC 11501 (SN69 ZRG) in a celebratory one-of-a-kind mosaic bus livery featuring the faces of customers, drivers and communities from across the UK.

Stagecoach South ADL Enviro200 MMC 37411 (YX65 PYF) shows off one of the revised bus liveries and new company logo on Eastgate Street in Winchester. (Mark Lyons)

In 2020, Oxford Tube replaced its fleet with new Plaxton Panorama-bodied Volvo B11RLEs, such as 50425 (YX70 LUH). (Mark Lyons)

Stagecoach Western Plaxton Elite I Volvo B11RT 54243 (YX65 ZKC) arriving into Aberdeen in the yellow and gold longer distance service livery that is being rolled out across the various Stagecoach fleets.

A particularly striking livery for Aberdeen Airport Route Jet 727 is worn by Stagecoach Bluebird ADL Enviro400 MMC 10895 (SN67 WUW). The branding was subsequently cleverly amended during the pandemic in 2020 as the service connected with one of the vaccination centres, hence the slogan 'From Station to Vaccination'.

Prior to the coronavirus pandemic, Stagecoach Fife planned to start an autonomous, driverless bus service between Fife and Edinburgh during 2020. Their introduction has been delayed, but is scheduled to happen in 2021. The livery shown on the demonstration ADL Enviro200 MMC vehicle at the NEC in Birmingham during 2019 might not be the final version used, given the new liveries being rolled out across the fleets.

Stagecoach Fife ADL Enviro200 26353 (YX20 OFW) is one of five dealer stock vehicles acquired in all-over white during April 2020 seen on a special Covid-19 working of the X55 from Edinburgh to Dunfermline. It was photographed leaving the temporary terminus at St Andrew Square, Edinburgh.

The green and white version of the Stagecoach stripes was originally introduced when electric hybrid vehicles were new. Stagecoach North East Dennis Trident 2 Alexander Enviro400 Hybrid 12075 (NK11 DHV) in Newcastle on Route 39.

Stagecoach Gold in South Wales ADL Enviro200 MMC 26009 (YX66 WKF) in Cardiff centre.

Transdev Varieties

Seen passing York Castle is Transdev Yorkshire Coastliner 3632 (BT66 MVP), a Wrightbus Eclipse Gemini Volvo B5TL in its distinctive two-tone blue livery. The rainbows and additional lettering on this vehicle were part of a support message to the NHS for their dedication and hard work during the coronavirus pandemic.

Pictured in York is Transdev CityZap ADL Enviro400 MMC 2016 (SK70 BWN), one of a batch that entered service in 2020.

West Coast Motors Group Upgrades

Borders Buses former demonstrator ADL E40D Enviro400 MMC 11801 (YX67 UZB) was pictured arriving in Waterloo Place, Edinburgh, on branded service X62 from Melrose. The company have an app where it is possible to track their bike-friendly buses. Initially, the intention was to feature two bikes per vehicle, but based on passenger feedback space was quickly expanded to carry four.

Borders Buses ADL E40D Enviro400 MMC 12008 (YX20 ODU) passes Sheriffhall in Edinburgh on service X95 but displaying branding for service X62, with suitable information about bike spaces included.

Glasgow Citybus operate on behalf of ScotRail. Two specially liveried buses on a shuttle service between Glasgow Central and Glasgow Queen Street stations. One of them is ADL Enviro200 MMC 41602 (SN65 ZHA), pictured passing Queen Street station, which was extensively refurbished in 2020/21.

West Coast Motors in conjunction with Scottish Citylink operate Plaxton Panorama double-deck B11RLE coaches such as 11912 (YX69 LHM) on their Citylink Airservice between Glasgow Buchanan bus station and Edinburgh Airport. The photo was taken as the coach entered Maxim Park Eurocentral.

Developing Shades of Yellow in Bournemouth

The shades of yellow have changed somewhat over the years in Bournemouth. Yellow Buses Enviro400 200 (SN17 MTO) is in the latest bright livery stating on the side that the company is 'Filling your community with colour'. The bus is operating Route 3 and there is fairly discreet branding on it. (Mark Lyons)

Seen at Gervis Place, Bournemouth, is Yellow Buses Wildlife Bus Wright Streetlite DF 867 (HF14 BWY) featuring very busy branding for Bournemouth Parks Foundation and Kingfisher Barn Visitor Centre. (Mark Lyons)

Pictured in Gervis Place, Bournemouth, on Route 6B, Yellow Buses Wrightbus Eclipse Gemini 181 (HFO3 ODV) does not carry any specific route branding. (Mark Lyons)

Carrying purple branding for Route 1B is Yellow Buses ADL Enviro200 530 (YX12 AKP). (Mark Lyons)

Bringing Back the Liveries of the Past

As part of the 20th anniversary of McGill's operation in Inverclyde, ADL Enviro400 J8960 (66 XKW previously SN59 AWX) was painted in this special heritage livery – the original colours of McGill's of Barrhead. It was unveiled at a depot open day in July 2021 when it carried passengers to the event.

Resplendent in the Rider York style of heritage livery is First York Wright Eclipse Urban Volvo B7RLE 69374 (YJ08 XYO), shadowed by the medieval city walls of York.

To celebrate the 50th anniversary of West Midlands PTE, National Express painted a number of vehicles in old-style liveries. Looking every bit the business, despite being applied to a newer body type, is West Midlands Volvo B7RLE Wright Eclipse Urban 2102 (BX12 DDO), proving that old liveries suit buses of today. (Chris Cuthill)

A slightly more modern National Express livery is worn by Alexander ALX400 Dennis Trident 2 West Midlands 4125 (Y716 TOH). It carries the second variation of the then Travel West Midland's low-floor livery as it would have looked in 2001. (Chris Cuthill)

Another more modern vehicle looking extremely smart in retro WMPTE colours as applied to Metrobuses and Fleetlines in the 1980s. West Midlands Scania N230UD Omnicity 4780 (BU08 EHZ) was photographed in the centre of Birmingham.

The year 2020 saw the 40th anniversary of the Stagecoach company, founded in Walnut Grove, Perth. By way of celebration, Stagecoach Fife Plaxton Elite-bodied Volvo B9R 53722 (SV11 FSC) was painted in the original style of white and striped livery and was pictured in St Andrew Square en route to Perth on service X56.

Looking very smart is Arriva Kent Thameside Wright Micro Hybrid StreetLite DF4301 (GN15 CWX) after its repaint into 1970s-style London Country Bus green to celebrate the 50th anniversary of the formation of the company during 2020. The bus, as seen here, was to later gain lettering above the windows noting the anniversary. (Mark Lyons)

The Red Arrow identity was well known in London for many years. Go-London Mercedes-Benz O530 Citaro MEC50 (BT09 GPJ) was painted into retro Red Arrow-style livery and was pictured heading into the bus station at Victoria.

Despite its rather modern curves, London General Wright NBFL LT150 (LTZ 1050) looks extremely smart in original London General red, cream and silver.

Another retro London General livery of red, silver and white is worn by Wright NBFL LT160 (LTZ 1060).

The last surviving Wright NBFL from a few painted in a retro silver, red and black livery is Metroline LT190 (LTZ 1190), seen at Christmastime on Oxford Street.

Stagecoach has repainted ADL Enviro400H 12345 (SN64 OGU) in an approximation of London Transport's tram livery. It is branded 'Selkent Ambassador' and commemorates the 40th anniversary of the opening of the (new) Plumstead garage. (Mark Lyons)

National Express Xplore Dundee Wright Renown Volvo B10BLE 62138 (X617 NSS) wore a heritage, traditional-style Dundee Corporation Transport livery, and very nice it looked too.

Go-Ahead East 7111 (N21 GNE) is a Caetano Levante 2-bodied Volvo B9R in a livery that approximates the original OK Motor Services colours. The company operated in County Durham from 1912 until the 1990s when it was purchased by the Go-Ahead Group.

As part of their centenary events in 2019, Lothian Buses restored Wrightbus Eclipse Gemini 1 Volvo B7TL 701 (SN55 BJX) into the Harlequin livery it wore from new – albeit the bus was originally delivered with yellow front branding for service 3. The vehicle was not around long in the heritage livery as it was sold in 2020 and never ran in service like this.

Also wearing the retro Harlequin-style livery for the company's 2019 centenary parade was Lothian Buses Wrightbus Eclipse Volvo B7RLE 112 (SN04 NHC). Again, the livery was very short-lived though as the bus was sold on during 2020.

Another restoration, this time into an original Airlink livery, is Lothian Buses Plaxton President Dennis Trident 664 (SN04 AAJ), pictured at Lathalmond Bus Museum in Fife during an open weekend in 2019.

First Leicester Wright Eclipse Gemini Volvo 32646 B7TL (KP54 AZL) wearing a simple but very stylish heritage livery, depicted as Leicester City Transport 46 at Humberstone Gate, Leicester. (Mark Lyons)

Another event in 2019 was the celebration of 125 years of municipal transport in Glasgow. Three buses were painted in retro liveries. Greater Glasgow PTE-liveried Wright Eclipse Gemini Volvo B9TL 37751 (SF09 LFB) is in the centre of Glasgow providing shuttle bus services during the celebration events.

One of the other vehicles to be painted in retro livery – orange Strathclyde Buses colours – was Wright Eclipse Gemini Volvo B7TL 32675 (LK55 ACO), arriving into a wet Glasgow centre on Route 57A. Sadly the vehicle was lost to severe fire damage in March 2021 when two buses burst into flames at the First Bus site on Cathcart Road.

Looking superb in the streets of Edinburgh is Stagecoach Fife ADL Trident Enviro400 19666 (SP60 DPK) in retro 1980s Scottish Bus Group Ayres red and cream Fife Scottish livery to celebrate Dunfermline depot's 100th anniversary in 2018.

Another old livery working extremely well on a modern bus is Stagecoach West Scotland Scania ADL Enviro300 KC689 (VCS 376), marking the 85th anniversary of Western SMT.

Liveries to Mark Special Occasions and Special Bus Features

In addition to the many vinyl all-over advertising wraps buses regularly receive, there are occasions when local special liveries are required. Lothian Buses ADL Enviro400XLB Volvo B8L 1125 (SJ19 OZD) is seen approaching Sleigh Drive in Edinburgh on service 25 in the very attractive special centenary design it received in 2019 for the company's 100th birthday celebrations.

Stagecoach were also celebrating the centenary of Devon General Buses, and ADL Enviro400 Scania N230UD 15893 (WA13 GDX) wore a not too dissimilar livery to the Lothian vehicle. (Andrew Chalmers)

On service 26, Lothian Buses Wrightbus Gemini 2-bodied Volvo B9TL 417 (BN64 CRX) approaches Musselburgh promoting the Platinum Edition 2020 70th anniversary of the Royal Edinburgh Military Tattoo. The design was intended to give a 3D impression of platinum. Sadly, due to the coronavirus pandemic, the Tattoo was cancelled.

In recent years, many operators have decorated buses in special poppy liveries for Remembrance Sunday. Lothian Buses Wrightbus-bodied Volvo B5LH 551 (SA15 VUB) has spent a significant amount of its life in a white-based livery. During 2017 to 2021 it carried three variations of Poppy Scotland messages.

In 2021, Go-Ahead North East Wright Gemini 2 Volvo B9TL 6050 (NK12 GDE), promoting 'Bringing communities together ... celebrating diversity', had an internal refurbishment complementing its already colourful repaint with retrimmed seats in a retro rainbow moquette featuring not only rainbow-coloured seat headrests, but also rainbow USB charging points.

Lothian Buses operate Wrightbus Gemini 3 hybrid Volvo B5TL 584 (SJ67 MGV) in striking merging rainbow colours for Pride Edinburgh. During its time in livery the bus has worked from Longstone and Deans depots, meaning that it has been seen widely across Edinburgh and West Lothian.

National Express also have a Pride bus: West Midlands ADL Enviro400 4905 (BX13 JWE), although it transferred briefly to Xplore Dundee during 2019 for their Pride events. It is seen by the impressive Birmingham Bullring.

Plymouth CityBus 509 (WF63 LYT) decorated in a Mayflower 400 2020 events design commemorating the journey of the *Mayflower*. (Alistair Train)

Go-South Coast operate a Stonehenge Tour and looking extremely attractive and freshly painted is ADL Enviro400 MMC 1636 (HF66 CFE). (Mark Lyons)

Fresh from its wraps for Lothian Buses 100th birthday (see page 84), ADL Enviro400 XLB Volvo B8L 1125 (SJ19 OZD) was revinyled in a stunning giraffe design during 2021 for Edinburgh Zoo to coincide with the recent arrival of the first giraffes there in some years.

Liveries for Hybrids, Electric and Gas Buses

As the bus industry moves away from traditional fuel-powered vehicles, this section looks at some specific examples of the buses that are now becoming the norm. Some hybrids have already been featured in previous sections. Brighton & Hove ADL Enviro400 MMC 319 (YX69 NWG), named *Reginald Noyce*, is in Live & Breathe livery promoting zero emissions and the fact that it is an extended range electric bus.

Ember operate an all-electric coach service between Edinburgh and Dundee using two Yutong TCe12 vehicles, which are charged up at the Dundee terminal point. Seen setting off from Regent Road in Edinburgh is YD70 CHX.

McGill's are investing in Pelican Yutong electric buses such as this yet unnumbered and unregistered example, which was on display at the company's Greenock depot open day in July 2021.

For a number of years Aberdeen took part in fuel cell trials, with buses split between Stagecoach Bluebird and First Aberdeen. During 2020, First Aberdeen took delivery of a batch of Wright StreetDeck FCEV Volvo Hydrogen zero-emission deckers such as 39703 (SV70 BWM). The project has been part funded by Aberdeen City Council.

Metroline BYD1475 (LJ16 EZR) is a BYD Auto K8SR electric bus, seen on what was its regular working on service 98. The livery has been used on a number of clean air hybrids and clean air buses in London.

A Yutong Pelican E10 demonstrator electric bus in London livery was displayed and trialled at the Coach & Bus UK 2019 event at the Birmingham NEC.

Go-Ahead London ADL BYD Electric E200 MMC SEe10 (LJ16 NNR) shows off its special branding on Route 521, leaving London Bridge bus station shortly after its delivery.

Tower Transit trialled Optare Metrodecker EV MD1 (YJ17 FXX), which also spent time with FirstBus, resulting in a sizeable order for First York.

The BYD ADL Enviro400EV is the new zero-emission double-deck bus using a proven combination of electric technology and batteries with stylish bodywork and passenger-centric interior. This demonstrator (now registered LF69 UXJ) has been demonstrated around the UK and was photographed at the Coach & Bus UK 2019 event at the Birmingham NEC.

Stagecoach Manchester 14014 (LF69 UYE) turning into Parker Street in Manchester. It is one of thirty-two zero emissions 100 per cent electric BYD ADL Enviro400 Citys, which was part of a £16.5 million investment to the fleet. The buses can travel 190 miles on a single charge. (Donald MacRae)

Stagecoach 14033 (LF69 UXN) is one of two electric ADL/BYD Enviro400EV buses that operate in Cambridge on the Citi 6 route to support the vision of an improvement in city centre air quality. (Mark Lyons)

First West of England gas-powered ADL Enviro400 City-bodied Scania N280UD 39462 (YN20 CCZ) is seen in the picturesque setting of Chipping Sodbury. (Mark Lyons)

Go-Ahead North East operate nine of these thirty-five-seater Yutong ZK6118 BEVG E10 zero-emission electric buses. They have been branded as 'Voltra' and are charged overnight at Gateshead Riverside depot via a DC fast charge connection. 8804 (ND70 AEV) passes Newcastle station.

First Glasgow acquired two ADL Enviro EV/E20EVs in January 2020 for use on route M3 (City Centre to Milton). One of them, 48902 (LB69 JKO), was displayed at Riverside Transport Museum before its entry into service. The livery reflects the partnership with, and funding from, SP Energy Networks and First Glasgow will receive a substantial number of further electric vehicles in 2021/2022.

Prentice of Haddington celebrated its 30th anniversary in 2021 by trialling BYD/ADL Enviro200EV demonstrator LJ68 CYO. It was pictured passing through Musselburgh on service 108, which connects Haddington in East Lothian with Fort Kinnaird in Edinburgh.

Lothian Buses BYD ADL Enviro400EV 292 (LG21 JDJ), one of four electric buses funded as a flagship project of SP Energy Networks' £20 million Green Economy Fund to enable Edinburgh to become Net Zero by 2030. The buses have been put to work on service 10 between Western Harbour and Bonaly or Torphin.